Native dwellings: the Northwest Coast

Bonnie Shemie

Houses of wood

Tundra Books

Also by Bonnie Shemie:

Houses of snow, skin and bones: Native dwellings of the Far North
Houses of bark: Native dwellings of the Woodland Indians
Houses of hide and earth: Native dwellings of the Plains Indians

Published in Canada by Tundra Books, Montreal, Quebec H3Z 2N2,

Published in the United States by Tundra Books of Northern New York, Plattsburgh, N.Y. 12901

Distributed in the United Kingdom by Ragged Bears Ltd., Andover, Hampshire SP11 9HX

Library of Congress Catalog Number: 92-80415

The publisher has applied funds from its Canada Council block grant for 1992 toward the editing and production of this book.

Canadian Cataloging in Publication Data

Shemie, Bonnie, 1949-
        Houses of wood
ISBN 0-88776-284-0

        1. Indians of North America. – Northwest Coast of North America. – Dwellings. – Juvenile literature. I. Title.

E78.N78S54 1992   j392'.36'008997   C92-090176-X

Printed in Hong Kong by the South China Printing Co. (1988) Ltd.

Acknowledgments:
The author/illustrator would like to thank Philip Hobler, Professor of Archaeology, Simon Fraser University, Burnaby, British Columbia, Dr. Wayne Suttles, Portland, Oregon, and Jennifer Carpenter of the Heiltsuk Cultural Education Centre, Waglisla, British Columbia, for their comments, suggestions and advice; the people at the McCord Museum and the libraries of McGill University, Montreal; and Bill Brenner and Claret Heider for their assistance and suggestions in the writing of this book.

The drawing on page 24 of the house of Chief Maquinna in Nootka Sound is based on a watercolor by John Webber done in 1778.

Bibliography:
Hawthorn, Audrey, *Kwakiutl Art*, Vancouver: Douglas & McIntyre, 1967.
Holm, Bill, and Reid, Bill, *Indian Art of the Northwest Coast*, Vancouver: Douglas & McIntyre, 1975.
Kane, Paul, *Paul Kane's Frontier*, Toronto: University of Toronto Press, 1971.
Nabakov, Peter, and Easton, Robert, *Native American Architecture*, New York: Oxford University Press, 1989.
MacDonald, George F., *Haida Monumental Art: Villages of the Queen Charlotte Islands*, Vancouver: University of British Columbia, 1983.
MacDonald, George F., *Ninstints: Haida World Heritage Site*, Vancouver: University of British Columbia, 1983.
Roberts, Kenneth G., and Shackleton, Philip, *The Canoe*, Toronto: Macmillan, 1983.
Smyly, John and Carolyn, *Those Born at Koona*, Saanichton: Hancock House, 1973.
Stewart, Hilary, *The Adventures and Sufferings of John R. Jewitt, Captive of Maquinna*, Vancouver: Douglas & McIntyre, 1987.
Stewart, Hilary, *Cedar: Tree of Life to the Northwest Coast Indians*, Vancouver and Seattle: Douglas & McIntyre and University of Washington Press, 1977.
Sturtevant, William C., ed., *Handbook of North American Indians, Volume VII: Northwest Coast*, Washington, D.C.: Smithsonian Institute, 1990.

The Northwest Coast

It was not light yet and the sand was cold beneath his feet as the boy helped launch the great wooden canoe. For the first time he was joining his father and the other men going out to cut down giant red cedar trees. His family was among the few who had the right to harvest trees. Now the time had come for him to learn the skill of harvesting and there was much to learn.

The chief of the village was building a house for his son who was marrying the daughter of another noble family. It would be a huge structure and would stand facing the sea alongside the important houses. People from other villages would come to help with the building and take part in the rituals that would end in a huge celebration to honor the house, those who would live in it and the children who would be born there.

This Kwakiutl village was one of hundreds of Indian villages that once dotted the Pacific coast from what is now Oregon and Washington, north through British Columbia, as far as southeastern Alaska. Protected from the cold Arctic air by coastal mountain ranges and bathed in moist breezes from the North Pacific, the people were blessed with a mild climate, abundant wildlife and lush vegetation. Not having as hard a struggle against hunger and cold as tribes further inland, they developed a culture rich in art and ritual, and built the most spectacular wood shelters on the continent. The first European explorers to see them were astonished that anything so large could be built by men using small handmade tools: they were particularly awed by the beautiful, and sometimes frightening, carvings and paintings – art that continues to fascinate us today.

3

Protected from the northern cold by high mountains, the Northwest Coast offered

idyllic settings to build the most spectacular wood houses in North America.

Felling the trees

The men who set out that morning were looking only for cedar trees, and the boy knew why. Cedar was prized above all other wood for its special qualities. It has a straight grain with few knots and can be split into long planks that are smooth and even. It is easy to carve but is also solid. When used in a house, it provided good insulation against the weather and its natural oils resisted rot. Tribes further north did not have red or yellow cedar; they had to use spruce and hemlock for their houses.

The boy listened as the men discussed which trees to cut. There was much to consider: where a tree stood in relation to other trees, whether it could be made to fall clear of other trees, and how it could be moved through the forest. They had no wheels, sleds or hauling chains to drag the huge trunks and heavy planks down to their canoes waiting at the seashore, only their own strength. More challenges would face them when they got home.

The village stood on a high bluff. The heavy load would have to be hauled up the steep slope, across the defense wall surrounding the village, and then to the site of the new house.

When a potential tree was found, a closer inspection began. The only tools the men had were chisels, wedges and adzes. The boy watched his father take a longhandled chisel, make a deep cut into the trunk and take out a sample to check for rot. The grain was then examined to see if the tree would make better poles or planks. Finally, when the tree was found to be acceptable, a ritual was performed asking the tree to give of itself and an offering was made to it.

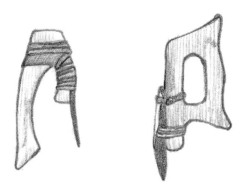

6 *wood and metal adze, wood and bone adze*   *stone maul, wooden wedge, elbow adze*

When all was ready, the tree was climbed and a rope made of twisted bark and wood fibers was attached to a high branch. The tree would not be cut down; rather it would be weakened and pulled down in one of two ways. The men could cut the trunk away by chiseling around the base, or they could plaster a ring of mud around the trunk a few feet above the ground and burn away the lower part. The men then pulled on the rope, directing the tree onto skid logs laid across a path pointing toward the beach.

The boy was given the job of cleaning the trunk of its branches so it could be used as a column for the house. Then he watched the men make planks from other trees: hardened wooden wedges were driven along the length of the trunk and carefully worked backwards and forwards, controlling the split. Sometimes planks were sliced off and the tree was left standing. In this case, an offering was made to the tree and it was "begged" for its wood. The boy noticed that care was always taken to leave enough of the tree intact so that it would not die.

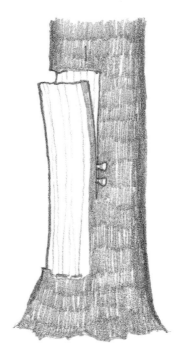

splitting planks

Posts weighing several tons were set upright and beams lifted into place

by men using only small handmade tools, human strength and ingenuity.

Building a house

The boy felt very proud as they entered the bay singing, towing the logs behind their canoes. He was glad to be coming home to his family and the celebrations. In the distance he could see the huge heads painted on the front of the houses, the eyes staring out. By the time they reached the shore, everyone was down to welcome them. Tomorrow they would face the hard pull to get the logs up the cliff, but tonight there would be a feast.

His village stood on a high bluff, protected from the surf and high winds of the sea by the bay. Log barricades and piles of rocks helped defend the village in case of attack.

The village was typical of those along the coast. They were usually on bays or inlets, in narrow valleys, or on high land, with the huge houses in one, two or three rows facing the water. Some had wooden decks in front for looking out toward the ocean or socializing, and sometimes wooden walkways linked the houses.

The dimensions of a house were first staked out with ropes and sticks. In the houses of chiefs in some tribes, floors were excavated in descending steps. This was done with digging sticks and baskets before the house was built. The different levels showed that the owner had performed acts of heroism and generosity. Levels were faced with wood planks. If they were deep, ladders connected one to another.

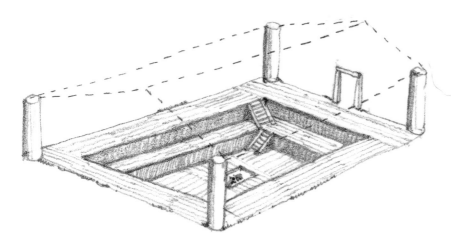

10 *excavated floors in the chief's house*

Holes were dug to the depth of a man's waist for the columns that would support the walls and roof. In the largest houses of the central and northern tribes, these posts weighed several tons and were as much as five or six feet in diameter. They were adzed into smooth poles, sometimes even carved with clan crests. Many strong men were needed to roll the logs into position over a hole and set them upright, pulled by ropes and braced with logs. Beams to hold the roof were lifted into place the same way. Finally, dirt was packed in around the holes to steady the posts.

Building the walls required yet more skill. The planks used might be as wide as five feet and as thick as five inches – a size almost impossible to find today because trees that old and massive are rare. The wall had to be built in such a way that it could be taken down and used in other dwellings during different seasons of the year. Planks were set on their sides, overlapped like shingles and tied to poles. Or they were set upright and slotted into the beams at top and bottom. There were no windows. Roofs were covered with loose planks, weighed down by rocks and logs. When a fierce storm came up the men rushed out to help hold them in place. One or more firepits for warmth and cooking were dug in the center of the building, and smoke holes were left in the roof directly overhead. Each hole was covered by a plank that could be moved with the aid of a pole to allow smoke to escape.

a Kwakiutl village

Clan symbols of real and mythical beasts decorated many Kwakiutl homes.

13

Houses on the central part of the coast were thought to be almost alive.

Styles of houses

Each of the tribes who lived, traded and warred with each other on the Northwest Coast had its own customs, language and style of house.

In the southern region, from Vancouver Island down as far as southern Oregon, houses were usually very large and sheltered many related families. One house might serve a whole community. A house still standing in Washington State in 1850 was reported to be nearly 1500 feet (almost half a kilometer) long. The most common house was designed like an enormous shed, its wide front wall left undecorated. Roofs varied: gigantic feast houses might have mansard-style roofs, others pitched. Inside, the floors were usually bare, parched earth. The walls were lined with cattails and woven mats to make the building snug in winter. Each family area was separated from the one next to it by rush mats.

In the northern region, from the Queen Charlotte Islands up to southeastern Alaska, houses were smaller and more tightly built because of the colder weather. They were square, averaging forty feet, and were built close together, often adjoining. Six beams on a massive frame held the roof planks securely in place, although sometimes only two beams might be used. But what made them famous around the world were the totem poles that stood at the front entrances.

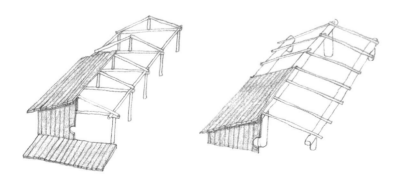

14 *southern style*

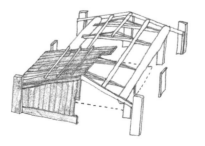

northern style

The art of the Northwest Coast peoples that dazzled the first Europeans and continues to fascinate us to this day was not mere decoration. It was their religion, the history of their tribe, and on a house, it announced the social status of the chief who lived inside.

Tribes who inhabited the central region of the coast from Vancouver Island to the Queen Charlottes did not carve and paint frontal poles like those further north. Instead, they painted huge murals over the front walls of their houses, usually a family crest, proclaiming that the dwelling belonged to an important and powerful chief. One might enter through a fierce-looking mouth which seemed to warn that only worthy people should dare go in. Sometimes a door was made in the back to carry out the dead. Just as one had entered the dwelling place of the living through the front door, one entered the spiritual world by leaving the opposite way.

Houses were usually given names. This was done in a special potlatch, or ceremony, when the house was finished. Names could describe the location of the house or the weather while it was being built, such as "Mountain House" or "Cloudy House." Or they could describe generosity and welcoming, such as "People Wish To Be There." The house that the boy helped build was called "House Upon Which the Clouds Sound" because it was so big.

Houses on this part of the coast were thought to be almost alive, representing the soul of the clan living in them and all of their ancestors.

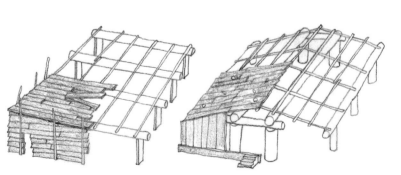

central style

Kwakiutl house front (circa 1900)

The giant totem poles of the Haida have attracted the world's attention.

Animal and human carvings represented spirits watching over the house.

Totem poles

Museums around the world compete to own totem poles from the Northwest Coast, and those that are lucky enough to have any display them prominently, for they always attract visitors.

Tribes carved and painted poles in many sizes and used them for many purposes. The most spectacular were those that stood as entrance poles to the houses of the northern tribes. Nowhere was the grandeur of the great cedars paid higher tribute than among the Haida. Some frontal poles were taller than four-story buildings! They were carved and painted with the figures of animals, birds, fish, insects and humans, in recognition of the spirits that watched over the house.

Each tribe had its own crest and particular animal symbols. A master carver was chosen, known for his knowledge of clan motif design and his carving skill.

He was exempted from other labor so he could devote himself to the work and was given helpers. First, the back and heart wood of the tree trunk were carved away to make the pole lighter and less subject to rot. Then the front was divided down the center with a line. The master carver worked one side and supervised his apprentices as they made a mirror image of his carving on the other. The designs combined the crests of the two families: the husband's and the wife's.

A hole in the bottom of the pole became the entrance to some houses. It was like going into the mouth or body of an animal. One was reminded of the ancestors who had lived there and the history of the clans. The poles were erected amid much celebration before the construction of the building was started.

18 *carving a totem pole*

Inside the house

When the boy finally entered his home on his first night back, only a small fire burned in the central pit. He found his family sleeping stall along the outer wall and gratefully lay down on his bed. Sleeping stalls were arranged around the outer walls according to rank; the boy was proud that his family's was next to that of the headman. Down the center of the building, the slaves were already asleep. Slaves were captured members of enemy tribes. They had no rights or privileges and were forced to work very hard, but they ate the same food and suffered no more hardship from the heat or cold than their masters.

Before his son's house was built the chief had collected everything his family had made or traded, and all the gifts they had been given. Now they gave all this wealth away in payment for work done and to show their generosity to friends. In this way the family safeguarded the importance of their ancestors and achieved greater power and authority in the community.

The house of a chief was transformed during the long winter. Elaborate theatrical and religious performances were given with beautiful costumes, masks and music. As many as 800 guests might attend. A platform was built and screens were erected beyond which spectators were not allowed to go. Acts of courage, magic and conjuring were staged. Secret passages and false floors aided the shaman in appearing to cut people in two and then producing them whole again. Some shamans used tunnels that led outside in their performances. These tunnels could also be used for escape if there was a surprise attack.

sleeping stalls

During the winter, the chief's house was turned into a theater for festivals.

Acts of courage and magic, with costumes, masks and music, were performed.

Houses in summer and winter

The Northwest Coast Indians lived in two or three dwellings during the course of one year. If one came upon a winter village in the summer, it would look like a ruin because the wall planks and roofs would be missing. They had been detached from the frame and laid across several canoes with the household belongings piled on top. The canoes then set off to summer locations. The walls were erected on the shores of rivers where salmon spawned and berries grew. Leaving the villages empty and deserted for a period of time allowed the weather, birds and animals to clean the site of fish remains and debris both inside and outside of the houses.

In winter the inside of the house was a busy place. Women looked after their children, cooked and sewed or wove mats. The floor was strewn with chests, bags and baskets full of stored food, clothing and equipment.

Suspended from beams were racks of drying fish, hunting equipment and cradles. Near the fire were boiling boxes and utensils for cooking food and smoking fish and meat. On the wall were darts, lances, poles, fishing nets, lines and hooks. Sleeping cubicles were sectioned off with mats or wood screens. Some might even have their own roofs. The bigger the dwelling, the greater the prestige of those who lived in it.

shaman's rattle

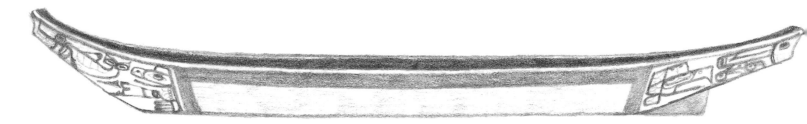

Haida canoe

Other uses of wood

Almost everything made by the peoples of the Northwest Coast was of wood or bark – houses, canoes, eating trays, storage boxes, food utensils, masks, hunting equipment, room dividers, mats, baskets and even rope.

Skillfully made wooden boxes were used not only for storage but even for cooking. These boiling boxes were filled with water and food. Then hot stones from the fire were carefully dropped inside, causing the water to boil.

Even clothing was made of wood fiber. A woman first shredded and soaked the inner bark of cedar. Then she beat it with paddles to soften it. The fibers were combed and then rolled on her thigh to make a tight thread. Threads were then woven into textiles on a wooden frame. Clothes were a loose shawl tied over one shoulder, and a cloak in winter. They were warm and comfortable and water resistant, especially if painted with ochre mixed with fish oils.

Cedar and salmon not only provided the Northwest Coast Indians with shelter and food, but were the basis of their culture, religion and prosperity as well.

weaving with shredded cedar bark

boiling box

23

Replicas of the great wood houses are being built by Native groups all along the coast as cultural centers, where people can preserve and re-create the arts and ceremonies of their ancestors.